LOVE YOURSELF FIRST, *Mumma*

COURTNEY LORKING

BALBOA.PRESS

A DIVISION OF HAY HOUSE

Balboa Press books may be ordered through booksellers or by contacting:

Balboa Press
A Division of Hay House
1663 Liberty Drive
Bloomington, IN 47403
www.balboapress.com.au
1 (877) 407-4847

Because of the dynamic nature of the Internet, any web addresses or
links contained in this book may have changed since publication and
may no longer be valid. The views expressed in this work are solely those
of the author and do not necessarily reflect the views of the publisher,
and the publisher hereby disclaims any responsibility for them.

The author of this book does not dispense medical advice or prescribe
the use of any technique as a form of treatment for physical, emotional,
or medical problems without the advice of a physician, either directly
or indirectly. The intent of the author is only to offer information
of a general nature to help you in your quest for emotional and
spiritual well-being. In the event you use any of the information in
this book for yourself, which is your constitutional right, the author
and the publisher assume no responsibility for your actions.

Any people depicted in stock imagery provided by Getty Images are
models, and such images are being used for illustrative purposes only.
Certain stock imagery © Getty Images.

Print information available on the last page.

ISBN: 978-1-5043-2055-9 (sc)
ISBN: 978-1-5043-2056-6 (e)

Balboa Press rev. date: 02/05/2020

Contents

Dedication

For my daughter, Jordyn. You made me a mother, and you made me realise how important self-care is. I love you, sweetheart. I'm so excited to watch you bloom into the most beautiful woman.

Preface

I bet you're thinking what does this chick who's only 21, and been a mum for under a year know about all this? Well, let me answer that for you, what I know about motherhood? Absolutely nothing. I'm winging it and praying to the almighty gods that every day I keep my baby alive. But what I do know is that if I don't keep myself alive and thriving then my baby, Jordyn, hasn't got a hope. So, Mumma, you need to put yourself first because like I just said, if you don't look after you, then who will look after your baby? Ding ding ding, that's right; no one will look after your offspring better than you. Do you get the picture? Now let's drop the excuses because we all have 100, I get it trust me, I got all of 2 hours sleep last night, and I feel awful! All the more reason to take a few minutes to make yourself feel better about it all, do you agree? I don't know why I ask you questions, it's a book, you can't answer me. But in my head, you're fist-pumping the air and saying YES COURT LETS DO THIS SHINDIG, so let's run with that!

You've got this, Mumma.

Welcome, Gorgeous Mumma!

Let's get into it shall we? First, I'd like to thank you so much for buying this book, for two reasons. One, you invested in yourself and well-done that's mega! And two, I no doubt did a little happy dance, and you made my day because someone wants to read what I've written? How cool is that? So, thank you so much, you're amazing, and I love you.

Well, I assume you're a mother? Or at least know someone who is a mother; who has given you this book to read. Did they just tell you to ignore all the bitching about the children part and the descriptive whinges about how nothing looks the way it used to?

Anyway, for the most part, I'll assume you created life within you and kudos to you! How cool are you? But goodness, aren't you tired? You grew a tiny human who took 9 months (really 10, but let's not get into that argument). You had so much extra blood in you which causes havoc on its own, your hormones were racing, and new ones were coming to life, and you HAD A FRIGGEN HUMAN INSIDE YOU?! That blows my mind, to be honest. You were either a pregnant unicorn and had no issues at all, your skin was glowing, you looked amazing in anything

Dear mothers, you'll learn to lower your expectations about what you can accomplish in a day. Some days it will be all you can do to keep baby safe, warm, fed, and loved. And that is more than enough.

— Anonymous

Pregnant Queen

Hi Mumma, congratulations, you have a baby in you (creepy, huh?) How are you feeling? Excited? Overwhelmed? Large and in charge? Feeling like you've been kicked in the vagina? Or maybe you're feeling absolutely incredible (Congratulations pregnant unicorn). My pregnancy was nothing but hard work, granted it wasn't by far the worst, I've heard much worse stories. But I was 37 weeks pregnant in the middle of summer, living in the Bronx (Not really but we lived in this horrible house in an awful neighbourhood, and I was so miserable and uncomfortable).

Totally not the worst situation (I get it don't come at me), but pregnancy is so hard at the best of time. Take this time to look after yourself. I know it's so exciting, and you want your babe here already but use this time wisely. I KNOW everyone is saying that to you and I get it you just want to see what this little thing inside you which thinks your bladder is a squeeze toy looks like, but take a step back. Realise you, need to get yourself in a functional mental space. I'm by no means trying to freak you out. Motherhood is the best thing in the world, and I wouldn't take it back for all the money in the world (and that's saying a lot because ya girl loves money), but it's such hard work. It truly is. So, let me start again. How are you, Mumma? Are you okay? If you're feeling fantastic about it all, that's sensational, and I'm so happy for you. But if you're not over the moon or not feeling how you thought you would, I get it. I had a tough time during pregnancy, and I wish I could do it all again because I genuinely feel robbed of the whole experience. By the end, I was in a much better headspace because I reached out. I had a mental health nurse come out to me every week; I needed the support. I wasn't doing well at all in my pregnancy, and I was terrified, not because I was becoming a mum, that was the only thing keeping me afloat some days. But because I had so much going on in my personal life and some old trauma coming back up (because hello hormones). The moral of this story is to check in with yourself, and I'll give you one piece of advice (only one because lord knows you don't need anymore) use your pregnancy to get you strong, take time for you and get your relationship healthy. Once the baby comes, things are going to be about them for a while, and the sleep deprivation doesn't do anyone any favours. I saw a counsellor every week, and towards the end of it, I got a foot massage almost every day because why not? I'm about to be someone's bitch for the next 18 years, abuse being alone while you can and enjoy it. If you don't check in with yourself now, that's when postpartum depression comes in, which you don't want (PPD can also affect the strongest of strong mummas, so I'm not saying that if your happy now you'll be fine, I'm just saying let's try and minimise the risk of you getting sucked into the black hole). Australia has so many free support systems around, use them. Talk to your midwives; they can point you in the right direction, and if you can't talk to them, go to your GP.

We had no money when I was pregnant (I'm not lying when I said we were in the Bronx), but we live in such a great country with an excellent healthcare system. Ask what's available. You may even be eligible for free relationship counselling if that's where you're struggling. It's okay not to have the fantasy pregnancy and not love every minute of it because your head in the toilet and your ankles are swollen. Still, it's not okay to be mentally hurting. You don't need to be. Reach out pregnant queen so you can enjoy this miracle of you actually growing a human, how friggen cool is that?!

Self-care isn't always about bubble baths and face masks; it's about removing toxic people from your life, changing patterns, and putting your true self first.

New Mumma

Hi Mumma, how are you? How are you coping with it all? It's okay if you're struggling. I feel like that is normal. You've just been given this little human with absolutely no instruction manual whatsoever and now you just need to trust your gut. You know what's right. Mumma knows best. It's essential to be kind to yourself right now. You're probably extremely tired, sore, feeling defeated, and that's okay. What's not okay is expecting you need to be some Pinterest mum with the most perfect, tidy nursery and a clean house. Babe, that isn't going to happen. Pick your battles. I want you to follow this checklist every day. You have two things to do every day, everything else is irrelevant.

1# Keep baby alive.
2# Keep yourself alive.
Sound good?

The washing can wait, the cleaning can wait, and do you really need to reorganise your wardrobe right now? No! Is the baby asleep? Go lay down. Go do something for yourself. Not baby daddy, not the house but for you. Rest, watch Netflix, EAT, shower. Something to make you feel alive and ready to take on what the baby has to throw you the rest of the day.

Courtney Lorking

Did you know in some cultures it's completely normal not to do anything for up to 40 days after birth, all the mother is to do is eat, sleep and feed baby? The housework is taken care of, meals are cooked, and family come and look after the baby while mum sleeps. I love this idea of support. That some cultures do, it is fascinating, but I know in my culture it just wouldn't be done. Plus, to be fair, I don't think I'd like to be surrounded by people all the time. Take ideas from this section, get your mother or friends to make you some frozen dinners that you can just heat up, ask for some healthy snacks to be prepared, and get as much rest as you can.

It's okay to ask for help too, reach out to your mum, best friend or Jenny from playgroup. You're not a bad mum for asking for help. I understand it can all be a bit much, and sometimes you just need 10 minutes to go have a shower in peace or go get some fresh air alone. I understand what it's like to be 'touched out' seriously I do, my baby WOULDN'T sleep anywhere unless on me and had a boob in her mouth, lean on friends and family right now. You must allow yourself to heal after birth. You need energy to be the best mum you can be, don't be a hero. Ask for help.

You're doing a fantastic job, my love, I promise you're doing just fine.

You glow differently when you are actually happy.

What the diddly is all this about?

What is Self-Care? Well, Mumma, self-care is something you do to take care of yourself. No one else, not your son, your daughter, or your significant other. They can be small tasks, big dates by yourself, or just anything that makes you happy. As a mum, our mental health gets put on the back burner and for what can seem like a pretty good reason (Having a little human or 4 depend on you for everything they do) but who will look after them if your rocking in the corner because you didn't check yourself? It's a harsh reality, but mums who don't look after themselves are doing their family a massive disservice because you are not the best mother you can be when you're on edge. Would you agree? No one wants to be the mum screaming at the child in the middle of the street because they have asked you for the 187th time can they have a chocolate cake. You will be able to handle every day stresses a lot better if you check in with yourself. (let's be real, it's really the kids that drive us up the wall, the guy who gave you cheek just comes at the wrong time, and he gets the full meltdown on your behalf, when it wasn't warranted.) Funny story I almost screamed at a lady the other day because she woke my daughter up, who I'd been trying to get to sleep for about 50 minutes, but then I checked myself and realised it wasn't her fault; how was she meant

Love Yourself First, *Mumma*

to know that? Not all of us whisper Court. But wow, would I have looked like a crazy lady yelling at this lady for asking me if I was waiting at click and collect? See this is why self-care is essential, not only do we all want to be the best mothers we can be but ideally, we don't want to end up in jail because we hit someone because we were on edge all day. It's harder to be a good mother when mummy is living in the big building with a barb wire fence around it. Jimmy will soon understand that it isn't a holiday spot.

Your life isn't yours if you always care about what other people are thinking.

Get Out!

Something I find really important and lifesaving to my mental health is leaving the house every day. Leaving the crime scene of the mountain of nappies, washing basket overflowing, and spew rags errywhere. Step out and just spend time with your babies for a bit. Nothing else matters in the world, but you guys, the washing will still be there, I promise (I mean I wish it wouldn't be for you, but hey, this book isn't magic). This tip may not be for new mums, I know the thought of leaving the house caused a mad panic within myself when I was a fresh Mumma. But now I am more established and somewhat have a routine happening, I find it so beneficial to leave the house every day. I'm not suggesting you go for a mega expedition; I'm suggesting you go grab a coffee at your favourite spot with a friend or go for a walk around the block. This is my favourite thing to do, and Jordyn, my daughter loves it too. Babies love fresh air and sun, its all-new things to look at. Every morning I grab my baby and my dog, and we go for a walk around the block, sets the mood for the whole day. For any new mum that's sitting there having a mild panic attack at the idea of leaving the house. ALONE. WITH A BABY, I get it. I see you. That was me, I don't think I left the house for about 2 months after my daughter was born, and that was after my mother forcibly removed me. I was quite content in my little bubble. So, do this when you are ready, start small and ask for help. Grab a friend and go for a walk. You have to leave the nest at some point, Mumma, and do it for you. Something that will make you happy.

Darling, you're a badass,
goddess, and you've got this.

Check-in with yourself, Mumma

Listed below is a checklist of a bunch of things that are considered self-care. I want you to get a highlighter, pen, or whatever makes a mark and tick or highlight the things you've done in the last week. If you get one or two that you've done, well done, you are off to a fantastic start. If you've done more, more power to you, babe! But if your page is looking awfully colourless let's make it a deal that you do at least one in the next week? Okay?

Moved your body, went for a walk or worked out.
Caught up with a friend and had a chat.
Took some time off social media.
Drunk two litres of water in one day.
Washed your hair.
Did a face mask.
Had a bath, by yourself.
Had a hot tea or coffee.
Ate a meal hot with two hands. (Roughly translated to without having a child crawl all over you)

I know some of these may sound really trivial, but these are just basic things we should be doing at least a few times a week. If you said yes to all of these, you're amazing, and there will be some more 'advanced' if you will checklists further on in the book for you overachievers (that is not a bad thing, that's a beautiful thing. You go, babe)

Self-care isn't just about holidays, massages, and walks. It's about working on your habits, mindset, and healing your past. It's removing toxic thoughts, people, and places in your life. It's living intentionally, purposefully and consciously.

Validate your feelings

Mumma, it's okay not to be the picture-perfect mum that society thinks it is the be-all and end-all. It's okay not to want to stay at home with your kids 24/7, it's healthy to have some time away and be your own woman. It's okay to want to go back to work, having something that's just yours and you can just focus on what you're doing is essential, career Mummas are amazing. It's okay not to want to breastfeed, just because the nurses say it's a must, doesn't mean you have to, you do what you're comfortable with and what works in your household. It is okay not to love your postpartum body, it's such a significant physical change, but you'll feel comfortable in your skin soon. It's okay not to love your baby straight away; if it was any other situation, you'd be called a fruit loop for falling in love in 2 seconds, besides you're so exhausted after labour and in shock. It's okay not to want anything to do with hubby after baby is born, you have so many hormones running around your body it's hard to feel stable, you're tired, and everything irritates you, and that's okay, this feeling will pass. It's okay to not feel sexy after becoming a mum, nothing is where it used to be, and you're exhausted. It's okay not to want to have sex for a while after having a baby, have you seen the way men handle colds? If they just went through what you went through, they would be down for the count for about 67 years, you recover in your own time, Mumma. It's okay to want 10 minutes to yourself, being a mum is the most demanding job there is. It's okay never to want to leave your baby's side, you're a protecting lioness now, you venture out alone when you're ready. It's okay not to want to leave the house or have visitors straight after having baby, you're in shock, and you want time with your family. It's okay to get frustrated with your kids sometimes, you're only human. It's okay to feel things Mumma, it's okay to not be okay for a second. You sit with how you're feeling, and you do you, Mumma, don't let anyone tell you otherwise.

I will not compare myself to strangers on the internet.

Reach out, Mumma

I see you, Mumma, hiding in the shower for 10 minutes break. I see you crying because it's all too much. I see you screaming for help but never asking for it. I see you being a fantastic Mumma for your baby. It's okay to need help. It's okay not to be okay right now. But you know what isn't okay? Letting it beat you. Making it take you. Reach out Mumma, before it's too late.

For anyone struggling, or know of anyone struggling, please know there is so much support around that you have access to. Well done for making a step-in self-care, but sometimes you need some more help, and that's okay. There is no harm in it. You are not a failure, you are amazing.

Please see the following list of numbers and reach out if you need them. Please also go and see your GP you have access to free help. These organisations also have some online support, so jump online if you're not feeling quite up for a phone call.

Beyond Blue - 1300 22 4636 (24/7)
PANDA - (Targeted for postpartum depression and anxiety) 1300 726 306 (Monday to Friday, 9am - 7.30pm AEST)
Lifeline - 131114 (24/7)

Love Yourself First, *Mumma*

Kids helpline (Targeted for 5 years to 25) 1800 55 1800 (24/7)
Mind spot (Not an emergency line) 1800 61 4434 (Monday - Friday 8am - 8pm)

*Please note these are Australian numbers. There will be something in your area if you are not from Australia.

I know it's hard, Mumma. I know it can be hard to get up every day and have these little people rely on you. I know it's hard to feel like sometimes your world is so small. I want to remind you; you are their world. You are the world that these little ones revolve around. You are their nurture, their home, and their comfort. You are everything to them, and I hope even on your hard days, you know how special you are. Especially for your little people.

—Unknown

Mumma Mantras

A mantra is a phrase repeated numerous times to create a positive thought process. Here are some great mantras you can repeat to yourself throughout the day when you are feeling a little defeated or just need to be reminded of the badass you are

Do what you can, let the rest go.
You've got this.
What do I want to matter?
I am human.
I am incredible.
I am a badass, Mumma.
I am calm and peaceful.
I can do this.
I am at peace in my own body.
My children are amazing.
My baby is fantastic.
I am an amazing mother.
Good enough is okay for now.
We have got this.
I'm doing all I can.
I am proud of myself.

Actually, I can.

Empty your bucket

You gotta tip out that bucket of tears before you drown babe. Let me translate, do you ever hold in your emotions for so long that one day some poor person who dares to poke the bear, unleashes the beast. You go into full-on meltdown mode. Granted, after you apologise to whoever it was that copped your wrath, you feel better. But wouldn't it be much better if we avoided the meltdown all together? Something that's really helped me and there are many variations of this metaphor bouncing around is empty your bucket. If you visualise a bucket and throw in all the emotional baggage you're carrying around with you this week; billy failed his test even after we studied all week, hubby was being a total knob, and that bitch at that set of lights cut you off. All these things you could handle separately, right? Together? DANGER! So, empty your bucket before you drown, whether emptying your emotional waste means having a little cry to your girlfriend over coffee, or going for a walk by yourself, whatever it is for you, do it. You'll be able to eventually tell when your bucket is getting a little too close to the rim for liking; for me, I get really frazzled and angry. Then I burn my toast and oh lord help up. Are you picking up what I'm putting down here, ladies? Don't cry over spilt milk (Unless its breastmilk, then weep like a baby, girlfriend) if we learn an outlet you won't need to schedule in your monthly breakdown.

Courtney Lorking

Much better for your health and if your anything like me, your bank account. Who else is an emotional shopper? Remember, little tears and time away is good for your mental health. Big tears and screaming matches with strangers, not good for your street cred.

Take time for you, Mumma.

Baby Daddy Drama

Romantic Relationships, alright before I pretend that I'm some relationship expert and what I say is bible, spoiler alert I am NOT. Anyone that knows me knows I'm not the best at relationships, and that's fine, so I'm going to just touch on this subject to hopefully shed some of my knowledge or lack thereof to remind you just how much people around you can affect you.

The bottom line, babies are hard work, and they take a lot of attention away from your relationship.

You need to find time for not only you but your relationship, or it'll just fizzle out, you'll be 55, your kids would have moved out, and you no longer have anything left in common. Because the only thing you've spoken about for the last 18 years was jimmy and how great he was at soccer last Tuesday night, get what I'm saying?

My relationship with Jordyn's dad is not by far perfect, we fight like there is no tomorrow, but we always remain civil. Not for us but for Jordyn. It's essential to keep the peace, but not to stay in toxic relationships also. You know what is right Mumma, sometimes having time apart could be just what you need. The biggest thing I have learnt in regard to your emotions is baby picks up how mummy is feeling. If you need to leave a relationship, you should feel no guilt because you are just putting you and baby first. Which last time I checked wasn't a crime? But you'd think it was the way some people carry on... but don't listen to them. Your baby needs two happy parents, whether together or apart.

I haven't mastered the 'find time for your relationship.' It's a work in progress, but here a few things we do as much as possible to remain a finely tuned parenting unit.

We would have dinner together every night. Put bubby asleep and then we eat together and talk about everything from how was the day to why is the colour purple called purple?

Date night, I've heard a lot of couples do this and have very successful relationships. In fact, I recently saw a couple that made a promise to each other, and it was every 2 weeks they would go out for a night, every two months they would go away for a weekend, and every two years they would go away for a week. Now they may not be entirely doable for some people for several reasons, your date night might turn into a date lunch with baby in tow, and that's fine. Your date weekend may turn into a staycation with baby, and your week away may be entirely out of the question. Still, you'll find what works for your family and your relationship. I think to have a lasting relationship with baby daddy (again disclaimer), maybe don't listen to me; I'll admit I'm struggling with this topic, but I think if you want to stay happy with him, communication is critical. On both ends. Talk about the issues you are having, talk about how we are feeling and what's going on for you and why you threatened to kill him in your sleep last night, you get me?

You guys are a team, you need to be open and honest about how both of you fit in baby's life and what is expected of you both. It's not all on you, Mumma. Daddy has two hands too.

*Don't wake up and think
about the mother you want to
become, wake up and be her.*

All the Single Ladies, put your hands up!

Single mummies, you guys are the REAL MVP. It's tiring; you aren't able to just tap out, sometimes your most significant accomplishment for the day is showering alone, which is mega, and I feel like that deserves some recognition. But some days, you may not shower, and that's okay. You're an amazing woman, and you're doing an incredible job. You are the mother unicorns, and you don't get enough props. If anything, you get handed nothing but shame and pressure. You don't need that, motherhood is hard enough, adding doing it on your own is just a whole other ball game. For the many reasons you may be doing this alone, you're not alone, and you never will be alone, you will forever have a little sidekick who you will both grow with. You should be so proud of yourself, and they will be forever thankful for everything you do for them. You ladies need self-love so bad; you never get a damn break, so please, take some time for yourself. There are so many things I could say, but there are too many individual scenarios about why it's just you and baby. But sometimes it's easier to do it on your own. I can relate to this. Your house is more peaceful because there isn't constant bickering, you do everything the way you want, and no one leaves the baby wipes open. I don't have any advice because you don't need it. This is just an amp up chapter for how much of a badass you are for just taking whatever set of cards life has dealt you and just handling it and putting baby first. I'm so proud of you, and your baby will be so thankful for all the love you pour into them. I hope you can find some time to give yourself a break, but I get sometimes it's literally impossible. Even if you can just step outside and take a deep breath. You got this, Mumma. You're amazing.

You are enough.

Friends, Family, and Fools

Relationships with people other than your partner, whether it be with your mum, your sister, your best friend, or Sally down the road.

Everything changes when you have a baby, whether you want to admit it or not. Everything from how you feel about your body now, your pelvic floor, and everything in between. Your relationships are changing left right and centre.

My golden rule and mantra I go by, my baby, my rules, and I don't change that for anyone. It's Bub and me against the world at this point.

What I mean by that is put you guys first, I am giving you full permission to say no to lunch with your sister because that's when bubby has her sleep. And no, you don't need to apologise.

I give you full permission to not go out with the girls because you would rather be at home with your son.

I give you full permission to say no mum, that's just not how I'm going to raise my daughter, and that's okay.

I also give you full permission to block, cull, and run far away from ANYONE who doesn't respect you and your baby. The most significant part of self-care is respecting yourself enough to put yourself first. Tina will get over the fact that you didn't get hammered on Saturday night because you have better priorities in life right now, and bonus points to Tina if she respects you, no questions asked, and lets you be. And a full blow best friend crown is she send you flowers and chocolates just because! Just because you've been friends with people for X amount of years doesn't permit them to treat you and babe any less. You're growing, so they either grow with you or respect you from a distance.

But you know what, if you want to go out with Tina and have a mum's night out, then you deserve that. You do you, and you go treat yourself.

The moral of the story is don't settle for less, you're going to change your priorities, your choices, and your idea of a great Saturday night. Surround yourself with people you love and run with then. I'm a big believer in you are the average of the 5 people you surround yourself with, so take a look at who you talk to the most, who you see the most? Do they inspire you? Do they encourage you to be a better mum? Or are they not someone you think raises your vibe or enables you to be the best woman you can be? I'm not at all saying get rid of people in your life because they aren't earning X amount or aren't married with kids like you're aspiring to be. But I am saying that you need to surround yourself with positive people who make you healthily challenge yourself, in an inspiring way.

Love Yourself First, *Mumma*

Find your tribe and love on them hard.

Moving on from relationships and how they are changing, the people in your life that love your daughter and you, whole heartily are the special type of people. The people in your life that let you bitch and complain about it all but then send videos of your babe laughing and say 'oh my god I just love this kid' and don't admit you to a psych ward because your change of tempo was just out of this world are exceptional. They get it. It takes a village to raise a child, and not just in the sense of, Mumma needs to shower sometimes, please hold this baby for me. But in the spirit of not only does a baby get born at birth, so does a Mumma, and it's all a significant change for her. Having love around you is what you need right now. If you're reading this right now and didn't instantly think of someone or a few people, then let's find that for you? You need support, you need someone to vent to and celebrate your wins with. We live in a fantastic decade of social media, and it's so easy to find friends at the touch of a few buttons.

There is an app called Peanut, it's like a tinder for mums, it's great. I highly suggest jumping on that and making some like-minded mum friends. You need a support system.

For those mummas that instantly thought of someone, send them a message and thank them for everything they do for you both. They may not realise just the impact they are making.

Delete, unfollow, unfriend, block, erase, and disconnect from anyone and anything that robs you of your peace, love, and happiness. Not just on social media, but in real life too. You don't need to be around people who don't see and appreciate your value.

I am grateful for...

Early wakes = Children to love
House to clean = safe place to live
Laundry to do = Clothes to wear
Dirty dishes = Food to eat
Grocery shopping to do = Money to use
Lots of noise = Kids having fun
Endless questions = A child who is learning
Getting into bed tired and sore = I'm still alive

- Chelsea Lee Smith

Promise yourself?

I need you to make a promise to yourself here, whether you change these to make it more appropriate to your lifestyle, then you do that. Still, I want you to stick to a list of a few things you will do every morning and every night. Some may sound a little trivial, but trust me, these little things that take no time at all (I get it, you're a busy Mumma) but do these things for you. These are the non-negotiable things that will make you feel just that little bit better every day. Do we have a deal? (Imagining you pumping the air and saying hell yeah)

Every morning I will...
Stretch (This will take all of 2 minutes, I do it in bed while my daughter plays next to me)
Make my bed.
Have a glass of water before you have breakfast.
Open up the blinds and let the light in.
Have breakfast.
Brush my teeth.
Get changed (Even if it is into another pair of loungewear, you just need to not sit in your PJs all day)
Breathe in some fresh air (whether it's just walking outside to check the mail, really just take a second for yourself and breathe in that fresh air)

Make your mental health a priority.

At the end of the day, you're the only one who can give your kids a happy mum who loves life.

Every Night I will...

Have a healthy dinner.

Have some water, *see later chapter on water consumption.*

Wash your face, really take some time here to wash off the exhaustion (Is that possible, no, but washing your face will help your skin, and just make you feel a little more human).

Moisturise your skin.

Shower.

Think of 3 things that you are grateful for today, even if you had the most horrible day, I bet you can find at least three things that went well, or that you are just so thankful you have in your life. This can make a significant change in how you saw your day. And will start tomorrow on a better note.

Turn the phone on airplane mode.

Ideally, I'd love you to leave your phone out of your bedroom and entirely away from you when you sleep.

Read a book before you go to sleep, I understand this can be hard in certain situations (babies in your room and you can't have light) but get a book light. Try not to watch TV or look at your phone for at least 30 minutes before you go to sleep (an hour is best) You may think you can fall asleep just fine with the TV going, but it can rob you of precious sleep.

* The last two are in italic because they are not going to be easy for some, and I don't want you to beat yourself up if you can't perfectly do all the tasks.

You are so very loved.

Headstrong Mumma

Word to the wise, don't take what any other mum tells you to do to heart. It seems that just because you have the shared motherhood hobby, every other mum under the sun seems to think they know your baby better than you do. They need to tell you exactly how to raise said child. Hell, to the no Hunny, back off. My advice, take everything anyone says with a grain of salt. It's not worth getting upset because Nora said you shouldn't dress your baby in blue because she's a girl. Nora, love, it's 2020, shush up please. Trust your gut, nobody knows your baby better than you do. Most women don't mean any harm by giving you advice, and if you feel like you're getting upset, maybe just check in with yourself and see why it's bothering you that someone is trying to give some advice? Perhaps you're tired of people thinking you can't do it? Maybe you're just tired, and I get that. But don't let one Mumma ruin your vibe. But there is a small portion in the mum club that must be that bored with their lives that they think it's their birth-given right to tell everyone how they should be raising their kids and what you're doing wrong. You can handle them two of which ways, I've tried both, and I suggest option A because it's a lot less effort. Still, option B is sometimes great because you're tired, Mumma, and you may need to unleash the beast to someone who deserves it. Option A, smile, and wave. 'Thank you so much! I'll give that a go' 'Oh that may work for your baby, that's so great Hun' and 'Thanks, I'll keep it in mind' all great options, shut them down quick before they start signing the adoption papers. Option B, a little less socially acceptable but, them the breaks.

Tell that Mumma where to go, tell her she has no right in saying any sort of unsolicited mothering advice and that you don't believe in her parenting methods anyway. Another good option, but if you have any interest in keeping these women in your life, I wouldn't give it a go. It's not received well. Moral of the story, focus on you and your baby, not what Jenny is doing with Tommy. Be kind to other mummas; you don't know how they are coping, check-in, and be that support system for them. And do not, I repeat, do not (this is not a drill) bring up any controversial topics, such as Vaccinations, your strong views on attachment parenting and breastfeeding, and anything else that may upset another Mumma. You have your opinion, they have theirs. Leave. It. At. That.

You are amazing. Own that shit.

Comparison Trap

Don't fall into this babe. Honestly, who is it helping if you are beating yourself up because Sandra's brownies are made with lentils? You are the best mother to your babies; do you know why? Because that's all they know, you're their mum, and that's all they want. Oh, and a handy hint, those Instagram mums are struggling with the same shit you are. They just have a better filter to hide their tears. This is something I think most mothers deal with at some point in their mothering days, if not every day. Feeling like less of a mother because someone over there is doing it better, someone's kid is walking before yours. I was big on not looking at the suggested timing of when babies should be doing things. This is one comparison trap that us mothers are the worst for creating. It really pissed me off when people would ask, 'Oh, if Jordyn not sitting up yet?' 'Oh, has she crawled yet?' Like no bitch, don't bring your pressure over here. She will do it on her own time and her own terms. Don't let Stephanie make you feel panicked, you'll know if something is not quite right, you have those Mumma bear instincts. One thing that helped me with this comparison, in particular, is being told that the babies that are good at the physical stuff are good at the physical stuff (Spoiler alert) but aren't as fast learning later on. Whereas babies that aren't as actively running around are more thinking about how things are working and why they are moving. Therefor better at the intellectual side later. Now, don't come at me, I'm not saying that they will be slow, but they might start reading or writing a week after another kid. And that's no big deal, right? So why does it concern you if my baby doesn't sit up when the little blue book says she's meant to? She might as week or two later, hell even a month (Drop the mic). Stop creating unnecessary stress for mums. We have enough to worry about like why hasn't my baby done a poo in a week, I'm not that concerned that she hasn't walked at 2 months. Trust your gut, and know that you are the only mother that your babies need. Mother them the way you see fit and don't apologise to anyone; you don't have to explain yourself to anyone.

Your kids don't need a perfect mum, they need a happy one.

Music-loving Mumma

You have to admit, you get a bit of a spring in your step when a banger comes on the radio or your Spotify. It gets you from feeling sleep deprived to badass Mumma in seconds. And that is the power of music. There is music for every mood, but my favourite right now is good feeling music that just makes you feel like a boss. Because Hunny you are, you're the boss at home. Music will transform your thoughts to 'Look at that washing' to Frick yes dance party in the laundry! Whenever my daughter is having a bit of a cry, and I don't know what's wrong (yep, I really didn't lie when I said I'm totally winging this mum game, no clue what I'm doing) but I just pick her up. We have a boogie and a sing. She's 7 months as I'm writing this, and she loves it. Music doesn't discriminate, every age can get among it. We've always got music going at my house, and I cannot believe the difference it makes in my day. Boring old housework turns into a one-woman show, lucky my baby is a baby still and can't be embarrassed... yet... watch this space. Wouldn't you rather your kidlets see you dancing and smiling and having a laugh rather than swearing that Harold ONCE again left the glass in the sink when the dishwasher is right there (anyone else feel like they are raising an extra kid with hubby included? No? Just me? Okay...)

Courtney Lorking

I created a Spotify playlist just for you ladies, its call Self love Mumma. Come across and get your boogie on with me. Trust me, you can't be more tragic than me? I dance like a baby flamingo trying to work out which leg is going to be the one, at least I own it and have the best time.

Love Yourself First, *Mumma*

Ten Steps to protect your vibe

1. Don't do anything that you don't feel 100% confident about.
2. Spend some time alone to reboot.
3. Avoid gossiping and putting others down.
4. Let go of things that are out of your control.
5. Don't compare yourself to anyone.
6. Ignore any opinions that don't add value to your life.
7. Keep your inner voice positive.
8. Stay away from energy demons (People who take your energy)
9. Be kind to yourself, things take time.
10. Put yourself first before others.

Occasional Self-love activities

Below are a few things that I don't know about you, but I'd love to do once a week (Goodness if only I had the time and money) But these are fun things you could do once a month or once every few months. Get out a highlighter and highlight a few you'd like to do in the next 6 months, just for you. These are bonus tasks.

Buy yourself some flowers.
Get a massage.
Manicure/Pedicure.
Treat yourself to a facial.
Girls weekend.
Go to the movies childfree, go watch something adult.
Take yourself out for lunch.
Get your hair done.
Buy yourself a new outfit.

All your kids want is you. Not the fit mum, the Instagram mum, the organic mum, not every other mum you think you should be. All they want is you. So be the best version of yourself, and you'll be enough. - OVL.

This or That

Below will be two different self-love activities that I'd love for you to pick. Grab a highlighter and highlight which one you would rather do (if you want to do both, highlight both, gives you more tasks to do)

Go for a walk on the beach / Go for a walk in the bush
Buy yourself flowers / Plant some flowers in your garden
Get a massage / Get a facial
Have a bath by yourself / Have a shower by yourself and wash your hair
Read a book / listen to a podcast
Go for a walk by yourself / Do some yoga
Get a coffee with a friend / Curl up with a coffee and a book
Sit in the sun at home / Sit in the sun at the beach
Meditate / Journal

Move your body.

Well done, Mumma, for wanting to move your body and get those endorphins pumping. My only requirement for you to start this chapter is you are either 6 or 12 weeks postpartum, depending on the birth you had and have had clearance from a medical professional. Other than that, let's get stuck into it, I promise your insides won't fall out. All have been designed in an easy to beginner scale.

It's imperative to warm up before training, especially if you haven't in a long time, so go easy on yourself, Mumma. You will slowly get better as time goes on, and you give it a red-hot crack.

Why you should warm-up before working out? Because warming up starts the blood flow to your muscles and gradually raises the heart rate. All of this will help prevent injury because what mother has time to be injured?

Before any workout! Warm-up, for 3-5 minutes or until you feel warm. Choose one or a few of the following options to get moving and warm, if you are unsure of any of these please head onto YouTube and see how to do them. Or find another way you prefer to warm up, this is all down to what works for your body.

Jumping jacks
Skipping
Run in spot
Side steps
High Knees
Kick unders

After every workout, you need to cool down, lower the heart rate, and stretch. Doing this will avoid your heart rate dropping too rapidly, which will make you feel dizzy and horrible. Stretching will help prevent muscle soreness in the coming days.

Spend about 5 minutes stretching out. You can find some great videos on YouTube about how to stretch. But here are some pretty basic ones you can follow below. If you have tight muscles and feeling a bit sore, get a foam roller and roll into that muscle, you can find a lot of great info on foam rolling online, I won't go into it here as not everyone will need to do this.

Don't forget to stay hydrated during your workouts. Please also stop if it hurts, stop if you feel unwell, don't push yourself. Your body has just gone through hell, be kind to it.

I have attached some photos briefly explaining how to do each exercise, but please if you don't feel correct doing it check out YouTube, just search for the name for the exercise, and it'll explain how to do it in detail.

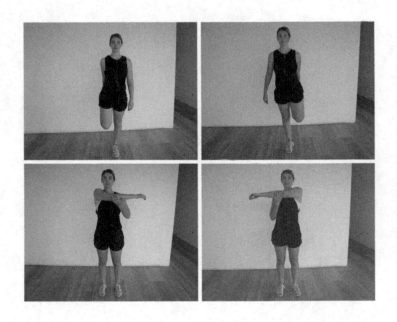

Work on you, for you.

Mummy and Me

Get baby involved or for the clingy babies #mychild –

Easy, beginner. 15-20 minutes of work. Go at your own pace.

Push up + Peek a boo - 8 Repetitions, 3 Sets (Translate for my newbies, you're going to do 8 Push-ups, have a 30 second to one-minute break, then you'll do another 8, another rest and then another 8, then move onto the next exercise)

Start with your hands just outside of shoulder-width apart, slowly release going down towards the ground, squeeze into your back. Avoid overextending your shoulders. Please do so on your knees until you are comfortable on your feet.

Squat and baby press - 12 Repetitions 3 Sets

Start with your feet shoulder-width apart, and baby at your chest. Push down as if you were going to sit on a chair, be mindful not to pull forward and let your knees go over your feet, you want to push your booty backward. Then come up and push baby up, squeezing into your back, and staying nice and steady.

Love Yourself First, *Mumma*

Lunge with baby - 12 Repetitions 4 sets (Change leg at 2)

Put baby at your chest, or wherever feels comfortable for you, step forward and bend at the knees as if you were being pulled down by your hips, avoid your front knee going over her front foot.

Courtney Lorking

Squat jump with baby tickles - 10 Repetitions 3 Sets

again, feet shoulder-width apart jump up squeezing the booty, coming back down with a slight bend in the knees for impact, then squat down and tickle that baby.

Baby Glute bridge - 8 Repetitions 4 sets

Place baby on pelvic bone, lock shoulders down against the ground, thrust up and squeeze booty and abs, and slowly back down with a slow release.

Seated baby twist - 12 Repetitions 3 Sets

Legs slightly off the ground. Chest up, shoulders back, slowly move baby front left to right, keeping your body as centre as you can.

Baby wall sit - Until fail once.

Place baby on your lap, lock shoulders and back onto wall, drop down until you are at a 90-degree angle with your legs.

Baby goes around the world - 10 repetitions 3 sets

Stand nice and tall, shoulders back, and slowly bring baby around, squeezing your abs to stabilise.

Stretch

*I give myself permission
to be myself.*

Mummy and me, carrier

Warm-up - Good warm-up idea here is also just going for a walk around the block. I know my girl loves this.

Place baby in carrier nice and centre and secure.

Lunges - 12 Repetitions 4 Sets (Change legs at 2)

Step one foot forward and bend at the knees and go down as if you were being pulled down by your hips. Keep your hips going forward and chest up. Then slowly back up, squeezing the booty.

Love Yourself First, *Mumma*

Squats - 12 Repetitions 3 sets

Feet at shoulder-width apart, bend legs, and push booty out as if you were sitting in a chair, avoid letting knees go over feet, back up with a big squeeze at the top.

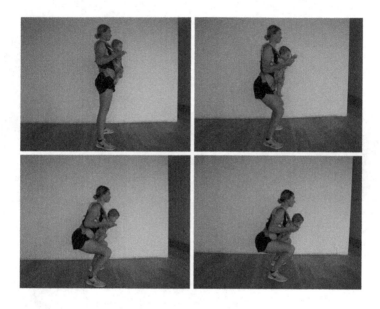

Overhead press - 10 Repetitions 3 sets

Arms out at a 90-degree angle, slowly push up squeezing your back and abs for stabilisation and down, coming down to a 45-degree angle and back up.

Tricep Dips - 8 Repetitions 4 sets

Find a box or bench, place arms behind you, knuckles facing out, slowly bend the elbows avoiding not to hyperextend your shoulder and back up with a big squeeze in the tricep or upper arm.

Standing oblique crunch - 20 Repetitions (10 all around, 10 each side) 3 sets

Stand up straight, shoulders back, and slowly lean to one side, squeezing the abs and back down, repeating and then changing sides.

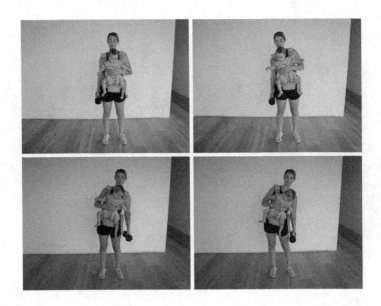

Wall sit - Until fail, aim for 1 minute. Go longer if you can.

Stretch

Place shoulders and back against the wall, slide down until knees are at 90-degree angle and feet are firmly in front. Hold until fail.

Stretch

It's okay not to have
everything figured out.

At home, no equipment

Warm-up

Burpees - 8 Repetitions 3 sets

Stand with feet shoulder-width apart, bend knees and place hands on floor, jump legs back behind you and lower body to ground, then back up and jump up and repeat.

Squat Jumps - 10 Repetitions 3 sets

Start with feet shoulder-width apart, bend in the knees, jump up and land with soft knees, then go into a squat with booty back as if sitting on a chair and knees not going over feet then back up and jump.

Walking lunges - 12 Repetitions 4 sets (Change legs at 2)

Step one foot forward and bend at the knees and go down as if you were being pulled down by your hips. Keep your hips going forward and chest up. Then slowly back up, squeezing the booty. Then step the opposite foot forward and repeat the same steps.

Courtney Lorking

Wall sit - Until fail, aim for 2 minutes but go longer if you can.

Place shoulders and back against the wall, slide down until knees are at 90-degree angle and feet are firmly in front. Hold until fail.

Single leg RDL - 15 repetitions 4 sets (Change leg at 2)

Stand with feet shoulder-width apart, hinge at your hips shifting all your weight onto one leg, slowly bend down with shoulders back and soft knee in the leg you're standing on, and straight leg into a T shape with the one going back, then slowly release the leg back down and repeat.

Leg raises - 10 repetitions 3 sets

Lay on back, slowly lift your legs until a 90-degree angle or as far as you can go, and slowly back down, not completely hitting the floor, then back up.

Love Yourself First, *Mumma*

Scissor kicks - 25 repetitions 3 sets

Lift your legs about 45 degrees off the floor, slowly cross one leg over the other, and then the other back under, squeezing and lifting with your abs.

Stretch

People are going to talk about you, no matter what you do so you may as well do whatever brings you joy and live your best life.

At home, minimal equipment

Warm-up

Shoulder press - 8 repetitions 3 sets

Bring weights to a 90-degree angle in line with your head, slowly raise up until the weights just miss each other, bring back down squeezing into your back and shoulders bring back down until at a 45-degree angle, and then back up.

Front Lat raises - 10 repetitions 3 sets

Have your weights in front of you, bring your shoulders back and tighten your core for stability, bringing the weights straight up until in line with your chest, then back down and repeat. Make sure you have soft knees, and your shoulders are back. Also, use a small weight for this as you bring the weight a very long way away from your centre of gravity.

Goblet Squat - 12 repetitions 3 sets

Having feet at shoulder-width apart slightly facing outwards, bring the weight in towards your chest, then going down into a squat as if you were sitting on a chair and then back up.

Lunges - 12 repetitions 4 sets (change legs at 2)

Step one foot forward and bend at the knees and go down as if you were being pulled down by your hips. Keep your hips going forward and chest up. Then slowly back up, squeezing the booty.

Mountain climber - 20 repetitions 3 sets

Place your hands just outside of shoulder-width or whatever is comfortable for you, leaving arms stretched out, bring knee up to your chest then back, and then bring the opposite knee up.

Russian twist - 20 reps (10 per side) 3 sets

Having a weight at your chest, bring your legs up, shoulders back chest up, bring the weight front side to side, keeping your legs up and your body as centred as you can.

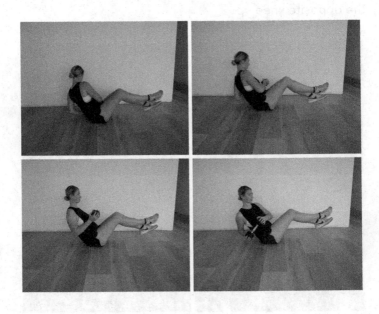

Stretch

Hating your body will never get you as far as loving it will.

Water you talking 'bout?

Water consumption - Depending on how much you weigh the average recommended daily water intake for women is 2.5 litres of water, how many do you think you had today?

*Disclaimer - Don't drink more than a litre an hour, don't go cheating the system. Your body cannot absorb more than 0.8 - 1 litre an hour. Slow and steady wins the race.

I have two tips for you, I used to be the worst at my water intake, so here's what worked for me. Get a cute drink bottle, get one you love to drink from, and you'll take everywhere you go. There are two benefits to finding a cute water bottle and reusing it. One; you love it, so you'll use it and two; reduce & reuse #savetheturtles. My second tip is to write on the side of the bottle an hourly break down, so if you have a litre bottle, you'll have to do two sides and remember to refill! So have 9 am, 10 am, 11 am and so on with little lines and by 9 am you need to have drunk up to that line, then by 10 am drink to that line. This is a super simple way to get in your water and stay accountable.

Love Yourself First, *Mumma*

Benefits of drinking enough water every day.

Decreases fatigue.
Increased mood.
Decreased confusion.
Boosts immune system (who has time to get sick when you're a Mumma?)
Healthy heart.
Working kidney (yay for built-in filter system)
Water delivers oxygen through the body.
Prevents headaches (As if your child doesn't give you enough of these)
Hydration = Glowing skin, anything to help those bags, you feel me, Mumma?
Supports the digestive system.
Maintains healthy blood pressure.
Supports weight loss.
Increase Brainpower (literally sip up, who knew the baby brain lasts well after the baby is born?!)

Wow, who knew I could write a whole chapter just on water, it shows you how vital I think drinking water is. Drink up, Mumma.

Fun fact, do you know the benefits of cold water? I finish my shower every night by turning the water cold, here's why...
Aids fat loss efforts
Improves Cardiovascular circulation
Reduces muscle inflammation
Boosts happiness levels

Courtney Lorking

Reduces stress
Improves Lymphatic circulation

If I ever have an anxiety attack, I go jump in a cold shower, it works almost instantly, it gives you a full restart. Try it out, Mumma!

Don't forget to drink some
water and get some sun, you're
basically a house plant with
more complicated emotions.

Eat your heart out, Mumma

Have you eaten enough today? If you had to really think about the last thing you've eaten, I'm betting you haven't. I see two problems with mums, especially new mums. You either aren't eating at all because your children eat first. Then you forget about yourself, or you get stuck under a sleeping baby, or it's onto the next activity to keep them entertained, or you eat the most unhealthy, empty-calorie food because you have to eat quickly between cries and that's all you can grab and eat? I've been both of these people, and let me tell you, it sucks. I get that being a mum is so time demanding, trust me, my baby doesn't sleep. But it's all about priorities and preparation. I was the type of mum who would finally get two minutes 'spare time.' Instead of rushing into the shower or grabbing something to eat, I'd check my phone to see what's happening on the gram. I totally understand that you want that two minutes of your time, and it's just mindless scrolling. Still, you're doing yourself a massive disservice by not prioritising your needs. Eat first, then shower, then scroll. Now, I go more into detail about preparation in the next chapter, so I'll explain that soon. But it is all about eating healthy food, that is all ready for you to save you time and save you getting into the chips (we've all been there). In the beginning, I do agree it's better to eat whatever than to not eat at all, couldn't agree more really. But you can have healthy snacks ready. Did you know that if you're breastfeeding, you need between 450 - 500 extra calories a day?! It's hard to get in any additional calories if you're not eating the recommended amount in the beginning. For those who want to know more about calories, the average woman needs between 1500 - 2000 calories per day, so when breastfeeding, it is quite a bit more required to keep your milk supply booming. Further in this book, there is a bunch of recipes you can make to have in the pantry or ready-made in the fridge for the week, so it's as simple as, grab and go. Fuelling yourself is one of the most important things, we need food to survive, and we need enough to thrive. You're already tired, Mumma, I understand. But don't put your body under any more stress than it needs to be because then you'll have more issues losing weight, if that's your goal and you'll be about 10 times more tired. Do you expect your car to run with no petrol in it? No. So why would you expect your body to operate when you aren't feeding it? Sorry, this was a bit of a Tough love chapter, but I feel really strongly about nutrition, and I'm all about mindful eating. Handy hint as well, for any of my Mummas thinking that if you don't eat, you'll 'lose the baby weight' spoiler alert you won't. You need to keep that metabolism firing to keep you and your body happy. Your body is a temple, as cheesy as that is. Look after your temple, it just birthed a baby, and possibly now feeding and keeping the kid alive. Do yourself a favour and keep yourself alive too.

*Taking care of yourself is a part
of taking care of your kids.*

Preparation is key

Alright before I say the word meal prep don't freak out on me thinking I'm going to ask you to prepare chicken mince, rice and beans for 5 meals a day, hell no. This book is about self-care, not how to form an unhealthy relationship with food, and mess up your body and hormones. I'm talking about food prep more so. What I found to be extremely helpful is prepping food once a week, so every Monday I do my grocery shop pick up (Woolies click and collect you da bomb, saving my life. Highly recommend if you haven't gotten on that bandwagon already) then we come home, I distract my daughter with her toys and dart into the kitchen to prep some food (I can see her from the kitchen, don't stress... it's all safe) but if you're one of the lucky ones where your child actually has naps through the day, maybe you can use some of that time to get your prep on. In my fridge, I always have a jar of cut up strawberries, celery, carrot sticks, and cheese slices. In my experience and the first few months of this motherhood gig, I wasn't doing this at all; in fact, I was hardly doing any grocery shopping at all. I was eating processed packaged foods, and ordering take away way too often. Not only did I feel horrible, I wasn't losing any weight, and it was so incredibly expensive. Having a few snacks at an arm's reach is so much better than reaching for those chips.

Basic Snacks.

Strawberries are a great snack when you feel like something sweet, add some dark chocolate if you want to spice up your life.

Almonds and dark chocolate chips are also a winner in my books.

Carrot and hummus, ahh, yes.
Biscuits and Hummus, yum!
Celery and Peanut butter, hell yes (Anyone else sometimes use the celery more as a spoon for the peanut butter, no bad Courtney, portion control!)
Nuts
Fruit salad
Trail Mix
Apple and almond butter
And cheese and biscuits.

These are all much easier snack options that will leave you feeling lighter, happier, and less angry because who has time to prepare a whole meal in-between baby cries?

If you're like me and have about 3 minutes to eat every day, it's all about convenience and being smart. Preparation is critical, Mumma!

Love Yourself First, *Mumma*

If you continue through to the next chapter, I have a bunch of recipes that are more advanced than a two-ingredient pair up. They are still very basic and easy to make, but you need to fuel your body, Mumma.

Recipes

Disclaimer, these recipes I've created aren't entirely healthy. Still, they are much healthier than a lot of options I know are more convenient. I'm all about mindful eating, and you need to be loving what you eat to stay on the 'Healthier' track. It's all about nourishing your body but also enjoying what you're eating.

Also, all recipes can be modified to be Vegan, Vegetarian, Gluten-free, etc.

They are just a rough guide of what I eat and enjoy eating.

Breakfast

Overnight oats (Cold)

Base -
3/4 Cup of oats
1 Cup of milk of your choice
1 TBSP Chia Seeds

Choc PB Banana
White Wolf Nutrition Protein (I use chocolate), Peanut butter and Banana

Peanut butter and berries
White Wolf Nutrition Protein (I use vanilla), Peanut butter, and berries of your choice

Salted Caramel banana
White Wolf Nutrition Protein (I use caramel), Banana and Greek yogurt, and a pinch of salt

Add base in jar, with protein of your chosen recipe, shake well.
Add in the rest of the ingredients on top, for example, add the peanut butter and banana and then seal the jar and place in the fridge.
If you want a fresher option, leave out the rest of the ingredients until the morning and then add the fruit in the morning so it's fresh.
Then enjoy after at least 6 hours after oats have been in the fridge.

Hot oats

Base -
3/4 Cup of oats
1 Cup of milk of your choice
1 TBSP Chia Seeds

Choc PB Banana
White Wolf Nutrition Protein (I use chocolate), Peanut butter and Banana

Almond butter and berries
White Wolf Nutrition Protein (I use Vanilla), Almond Butter, and berries of your choice

Salted Caramel banana
White Wolf Nutrition Protein (I use Caramel), Banana and Greek yogurt, pinch of salt.

Place base with your chosen protein from chosen recipe into a bowl and place into the microwave (Because let's just pick our battles here, I personally don't have time to cook them on the stove as much as I'd love to)
Then once oats are cooked, add the rest of the ingredients on top.

Then enjoy straight away.

Egg muffins

*Recipe makes 6 egg muffins
6 Eggs

Pick what vegetables you want
Mushrooms, Alfalfa Sprouts, Carrot, Onion, Tomato, Pumpkin, Leek, Potato, Capsicum, Sweet Potato, Avocado, Sun-dried tomato

Pick a green
Spinach, Broccoli, Zucchini, Kale, Asparagus

Pick a cheese
Feta, Cheddar, Goats, Parmesan, Brie, Haloumi

Pick a protein
Bacon, Ham, Chorizo, Beef mince, Chicken, Tuna, Smoked salmon

Preheat oven to 180 degrees
Add the eggs into a bowl, mix until combined.
Spray 6 muffin tray with non-stick spray.
Pour even amount of egg into 6 muffin tray.
Add in the vegetables you want into the egg mixture (cut into small pieces).
Add the green you want.
Add the protein.

Love Yourself First, *Mumma*

Top with the cheese you want.
Bake for 20 minutes.
Let sit for 10 minutes after cook thoroughly.
Garnish with lemon or lime and salt and pepper as desired.

*For added flavour you can pre-prep and pre-cook the vegetables you want to use in garlic or a seasoning of your choice. My personal favourite is mushrooms in garlic.

Omelette

---

2 Eggs
1/4 Cup Milk
Salt and pepper

Pick what vegetables you want
Mushrooms, Alfalfa Sprouts, Carrot, Onion, Tomato, Pumpkin, Leek, Potato, Capsicum, Sweet Potato, Avocado, Sun-dried Tomato

Pick a green
Spinach, Broccoli, Zucchini, Kale, Asparagus

Pick a cheese
Feta, Cheddar, Goats, Parmesan, Brie, Haloumi

Pick a protein
Bacon, Ham, Chorizo, Beef mince, Chicken, Tuna, Smoked salmon

Add milk and eggs into bowl, stir to combine.
Heat non-stick pan at medium heat.
Place a small amount of olive oil in a pan.
Place egg mixture in and let it cook until it started cooking.
Add desired filling into the centre of the omelette
Fold up the two sides into the centre covering the filling.
Flip over to allow the other side to cook.
Once cooked and brown, plate up.
Add salt and pepper, and lemon if desired.

Main Meals

Chicken Fajitas

Serves 4

700g Chicken breast
1 Yellow Capsicum
1 Green Capsicum
1 Red Capsicum
1 Small brown onion
1 TBSP Olive oil
Salt
Pepper
1/2 tsp Garlic Powder
1/2 tsp Onion powder
1/2 tsp ground cumin
1/2 smoked paprika
Lime
Coriander (Optional)
Tortillas

Preheat oven to 220 Degrees
In a large bowl, combine Chicken breast (Cut into strips),
onion (Cut in pieces) and Capsicum (Cut into strips), Olive
oil, salt, and pepper, and spices.
Stir and mix it all together, lightly coating the chicken and
capsicum in oil and spice
Place mixture on a baking tray lined with baking paper

Love Yourself First, *Mumma*

Cook at 220 for 20 minutes or until chicken is cooked stirring halfway.

Heat tortillas as directed on the package.

Serve with mixture in tortillas and lime and coriander on top.

Burrito Bowl

Serves 4

500g Turkey Mince, Beef mince or Chicken breast cut up
500g Rice of your choice (I use Basmati)
1 TBSP ground cumin
1 TBSP Paprika
1 TBSP ground oregano
1/2 Tsp Chilli Powder
1/2 Tsp Garlic powder
420g Corn kernels
420g Black Beans
300g Salsa
Grated cheese
3 Avocado
1 Red onion
1 Lime
1 Brown onion
Sour cream or Greek yogurt (If desired)

Place Avocado, cut up Red onion and Lime juice in a bowl, combine until a guacamole consistency.
Start cooking rice as stated on the package.
Place all spices in a small bowl and stir until combined.
Place your choice of meat and cut up brown onion into a frying pan with a small amount of olive oil. Mix in a

tablespoon of the spice mix (Store the rest in an airtight container)

Cook meat until thoroughly cooked and onions are browned.

Rinse corn and beans.

Place Rice onto plate, then add meat and onion mix, then add beans and corn.

Dress with Salsa, Avocado and Cheese to top.

You may add sour cream or plain Greek yogurt if you want also.

Chicken Pesto Pasta

Serves 4

500g Chicken Breast
Bunch of Basil (Roughly 2 Cups)
350g Penne Pasta
Salt and Pepper
1 TBSP Olive oil
1 Cup light cream
1/2 Cup Parmesan (For Pasta)
Bunch of Asparagus
Punnet of baby tomatoes
1/4 cup pine nuts
1 TBSP Garlic Powder
3/4 Cup of Parmesan (For Pesto)
5 TBSP Olive oil

Heat Olive oil in a pan, add in cut chicken (Into bite-size pieces) Season the chicken with salt and pepper to taste. Leave in pan until fully cooked and light brown in colour. Remove chicken from pan.
Place asparagus into the oven on a baking tray lined with baking paper. Top with a light layer of olive oil and salt and pepper. Cook at 200 degrees for 12 minutes or until light brown.
Cook pasta according to the package directions.

Love Yourself First, *Mumma*

Make pesto by adding Pine nuts, garlic powder, Parmesan, olive oil, and 1 · cups of the basil leaves. Blend in a blender until desired consistency.

Add pesto and light cream into pasta and stir well until combined.

Add chicken into bowl, and Asparagus cut up.

Stir in parmesan.

Serve with Tomatoes sliced in half and basil.

Chicken Buddha bowl

Serves 2

300g Chicken breast
1 TBSP Garlic
1 TBSP Paprika
3 Cups of rice
1 Zucchini
1 Avocado
100g Bean sprouts
Sweet chilli sauce

Place rice in rice cooker (Or as directed)
Cut up chicken into strips and cook them in a small amount
of olive oil, top with Garlic and Paprika.
Cook until golden brown.
In a separate pan, cook cut up zucchini in salt and pepper
until slightly browned.
Place rice into a bowl, add chicken and zucchini.
Top with bean sprouts, avocado, and sweet chilli sauce.

Tuna Pasta

Serves 4

300g pasta of your choice (Swap with Quinoa if needed)
4 Stalks of celery
1 Small head of lettuce
420g Corn
1 Punnet of baby tomato
1/2 Red onion
1 1/2 Cup of plain Greek yogurt
1 TBSP Seeded mustard
1 TBSP Lime juice
Salt and Pepper to taste
Tuna (One small jar per person)

Cook pasta as stated on package
Cut up Celery into small pieces, cut up tomatoes in half, cut up red onion into small pieces, and cut up lettuce to small strands and set aside.
Add Greek yogurt, mustard, lime juice, and salt and pepper in a small jar and shake it up, set aside.
Once pasta is done and drained, add the yogurt mix into pasta and stir through.
Add in the rest of the ingredients prepared early (Celery, Tomato, Onion and Lettuce)
Serve onto plates and top with tuna

Tofu Buddha Bowl

Serves 2

250g Tofu
1/3 cup Soy sauce
1 TBSP Garlic Powder
200g spinach
2 Cups of rice
2 Cups of quinoa
Avocado
Sweet Chilli sauce

Marinate Tofu cut up into squares in soy cause and garlic powder overnight or for a few hours.
Place rice, quinoa into rice cooker with rice.
Place tofu into pan, cook until lightly brown (about 15-20 minutes)
Add spinach and cook until liking.
Place rice into a bowl, add tofu, then top with avocado and sweet chilli sauce.

Chicken pasta Salad

Serves 4

500g Chicken breast
300g Spinach
420g Corn
300g Pasta
1/2 small red onion
1 Punnet of baby tomatoes
Olive oil
1/2 TBSP garlic powder
1/2 TBSP Paprika
1/2 Cup of mayonnaise
1/4 cup of Dijon Mustard
4 TBSP White vinegar
1/4 Cup of milk
Salt n pepper to taste
Sesame seeds and chilli flakes (Optional)

Cook pasta as directed on package
Cut up chicken into small strips, place in a bowl and add a dash of olive oil, Garlic powder, Paprika and salt, and pepper to taste, combine until coated.
Place chicken on a medium temp on the stove and cook until golden.
Cut up tomatoes and onion to small pieces.

Courtney Lorking

Place Mayonnaise, Mustard, vinegar, milk and salt n pepper into bowl, stir to combine.

Drain pasta and add to bowl with sauce mixture in, stir to combine.

Add chicken to pasta and add spinach.

Mix until combined.

Add onion and tomato, mix until combined.

Serve up and top with sesame seeds and chilli flakes if desired.

Chicken bacon avocado salad with lemon vinaigrette

Serves 4

200g Bacon bites
500g Chicken breast
2 Avocados
2 TBSP Chives
420g Corn
1/2 small red onion
1 Lettuce head
1 Lemon
1 Lime
1 Capsicum
400g Roma tomato
1/4 cup olive oil
Salt and pepper
1 TBSP Moroccan spice
1/2 TBSP Paprika
1 TBSP Garlic powder

Cut up chicken into small bite-size pieces and add to a bowl. Add in Moroccan spice, Paprika, Garlic powder, Splash of olive oil and salt and pepper to taste. Stir to combine.
Place chicken in frypan and cook until golden brown.

Courtney Lorking

Add bacon with a small amount of olive oil into frypan and cook until golden brown.

Cut up Onion, Lettuce head, Capsicum, Tomatoes, and place in a bowl with Corn. Mix to combine.

Place juice from the lemon and lime with the Olive oil and salt and pepper into a jar and shake to combine.

Add chicken and bacon in with the salad mix, toss to combine.

Serve up and add sliced avocado on top, drizzle with dressing and chives if desired.

Snack
attack

Salted Caramel
Banana Bread

125g Butter, Melted
1 Cup of brown sugar
1 Cup of plain flour
1 TSBP baking powder
1 TSBP Cinnamon
3/4 Cup White Wolf Nutrition Caramel Protein
Pinch of salt
2 Eggs
3 Mashed bananas
1 TSBP Vanilla extract

Preheat the oven to 160 Degrees
Place butter and brown sugar into a bowl and stir to combine.
Then add the rest of the wet ingredients (eggs, banana, and vanilla) Stir to combine.
Then add the remaining dry ingredients (flour, Baking powder, cinnamon, and protein. Stir until you get a batter consistency
Place in a lined loaf tray.
Place in oven and cook for 50 - 55 minutes, or until golden and cooked all the way through.
Cool in tin until cool and then enjoy.

Choc oat muffin

1 · Cups of Oats
1 Cup of Self Raising flour
3 Large overripe bananas
2 Eggs
1/3 cup honey
2 Tbsp Vanilla
2 Tbsp Baking powder
3/4 Cups of milk
1/2 Tsp Salt
3 Tbsp Cocoa powder
1 Scoop of Chocolate protein powder (I use White Wolf Nutrition.
1 Cup of dark chocolate chips

Preheat oven to 180 Degrees
Place wet ingredients into a bowl and stir until combined.
Add in dry ingredients except the chocolate chips, stir until combined.
Add in choc chips until evenly through the batter.
Place batter into a lined muffin tray. Will make approx. 14 Muffins.
Bake at 180 for 20 minutes or until cooked (Stick a toothpick into a muffin, and if it comes out clean it's ready)

Berry Muffin

1 Cup of plain flour
2 Scoops of protein of your choice (I use White Wolf Nutrition)
3/4 Cup of Coconut sugar
3/2 Tsp salt
2 Tsp baking powder
1/3 cup vegetable oil
1 large egg
1/2 Cup milk
1 1/2 Vanilla extract
2 Cups of frozen berry of your choice

Preheat oven to 180 degrees.
In a bowl, add in all dry ingredients. Stir to combine.
Then add wet ingredients except the berries.
In a separate bowl coat, the berries in a small amount of flour just so they are lightly coated (You do this, so the berries won't sink to the bottom when you cook the muffins)
Add in the berries to the mixture.
Place batter into the lined muffin tray will make approx. 12.
Bake for 20 minutes or until cooked.

Hummus

600g Chickpeas, drained and rinsed.
1 Tsp Cumin
1 Tsp Cajun
1 Tsp Lime juice
100ml Olive oil
1/4 cup Water
Optional (Add in a flavouring such as · Cup Beetroot or
Sundried Tomatoes)

Add all ingredients into a blender and blend until smooth.
Serve with carrots or crackers or anything you desire.

Honey Nut Granola

---

4 Cups of Oats
1 Cup Chopped Pecans
1 Cup Chopped Almonds
2 TBSP Brown sugar
1 TBSP Cinnamon
1/2 Cup Melted Butter
1/2 Cup Honey
1 Scoop White Wolf Nutrition Salted Caramel Protein

Preheat oven to 200 Degrees.
In a large bowl, mix all the dry ingredients together.
In a smaller bowl mix all the wet ingredients together
Add the wet mixture to the dry and combine
Line a baking tray with baking paper and spread out mixture onto the paper.
Place in oven for 10 minutes, stir, then cook for a further 15 minutes or until golden.

Protein Balls

White Choc Macadamia

---

1 Cup of oat flour
2/3 Cup of dried coconut
3 TBSP almond butter
2 Tsp Vanilla extract
1 Cup of Macadamias
1/4 Cup white choc chips
1 Scoop vanilla protein (I use White Wolf Nutrition)
2 TBSP Coconut oil
8 Dates

Put all ingredients into blender and blend until mixed.
Roll into balls and place them in a container and into the
fridge for at least 2 hours.

Choc Peanut butter

---

1 Cup oats
2 TBSP Honey or Agave nectar
1 Scoop White Wolf Nutrition Protein of your choice
1 Cup Peanut Butter
1 TBSP Vanilla Essence
1 TBSP Chia Seeds
2 TBSP Cocoa Powder
2 TBSP Coconut Oil

Put all ingredients into blender and blend until mixed.
Roll into balls and place them in a container and into the
fridge for at least 2 hours.

Salted caramel

- 8 Pitted dates
1/4 TSP salt
1 Cup of almonds
1 1/2 scoop of White Wolf Nutrition caramel protein
2 TBSP Coconut oil
1 TBSP Honey

Put all dry ingredients into blender, blend until fine
Add the rest of the ingredients and blend until mixed.
Roll into balls and place them in the fridge for 2-3 hours.

Lamington

2 TBSP cocoa powder
12 Pitted dates
2 TBSP coconut oil
1 cup almond meal
1 TBSP Chia seeds
1/2 cup shredded Coconut
1 Scoop of White wolf Nutrition protein of your choice

Put all dry ingredients into blender, blend until fine
Add the rest of the ingredients and blend until mixed.
Roll into balls and roll in the coconut until evenly covered
and place in the fridge for 2-3 hours.

Lemon Coconut

1 Cup Cashew Butter
1 TBSP Honey
1 Cup Almond Flour
1/2 TBSP Vanilla Essence
Juice from One Lemon
Zest from One Lemon
1 Scoop White Wolf Nutrition Protein of your choice
1 TBSP Coconut oil
1/4 cup shredded Coconut

Place all ingredients into a blender, blend until all combined and roll into balls.
Roll the balls into the coconut and then place it in a container and in the fridge for at least 2 hours to set.

Smoothies

Cinnamon roll smoothie

A cup of milk of your choice (I use almond milk)
1/2 cup of Vanilla Greek Yogurt
1/2 cup of Oats
4 Pitted dates
1/2 TBSP cinnamon
1 Frozen banana
1 scoop of White Wolf Nutrition protein (I use Caramel)

Put all ingredients into a blender and blend until smooth, add ice if you want a colder finish or if you want it more Frappe style.

Choc peanut butter bonza

1 Scoop of White Wolf Nutrition protein (I use Chocolate)
1 TBSP Cocoa Powder
2 TBSP Peanut butter
1 Frozen Banana
2 Cups of milk of your choice

Put all ingredients into a blender and blend until smooth, add ice if you want a colder finish or if you want it more Frappe style.

You're so busy doubting yourself
that you don't realise what an
incredible mother you are.

Choc cherry chiller

1 Scoop of White Wolf Nutrition protein (I use chocolate)
1/2 TBSP Cocoa Powder
2 Cups of Frozen Cherries
1 TBSP of dark choc nibs
1 1/2 cups of milk of your choice

Put all ingredients into a blender and blend until smooth, add ice if you want a colder finish or if you want it more Frappe style.

Bananarama

1 scoop of White Wolf Nutrition protein (I use Vanilla)
1 Frozen Banana
2 TBSP almond butter
1 TBSP of honey
1 1/2 cups of milk of your choice

Put all ingredients into a blender and blend until smooth, add ice if you want a colder finish or if you want it more Frappe style.

Mocha, wake up call

1 scoop of White Wolf Nutrition Protein of your choice
1 TBSP Instant coffee or shot of coffee whichever is your
preference. I'm a basic bitch when it comes to coffee.
2 TBSP of cocoa
1/2 Avocado
1 1/2 cups of milk of your choice

Put all ingredients into a blender and blend until smooth,
add ice if you want a colder finish or if you want it more
Frappe style.

Coffee in hand, confidence in the other.

Very berry vanilla

1 scoop of White Wolf Nutrition protein (I use Vanilla)
2 Cups of frozen berries of your choice
1/2 cup of Greek yogurt
Handful of Spinach
1 TBSP olive oil
1 1/2 cups of milk of your choice

Put all ingredients into a blender and blend until smooth, add ice if you want a colder finish or if you want it more Frappe style.

Pina colada

1 Scoop of White Wolf Nutrition protein (I use Vanilla)
1 Frozen banana
1 Cup of frozen pineapple
1 Scoop of Coconut yogurt
1 1/2 Milk of your choice (I use coconut milk)

Put all ingredients into a blender and blend until smooth, add ice if you want a colder finish or if you want it more Frappe style.

Salted Caramel? Hooray!

1 Scoop of White Wolf Nutrition Protein (I use caramel)
1 Frozen banana
Pinch of salt
1/2 TBSP cinnamon
4 Pitted dates
1 1/2 Milk of your choice

Put all ingredients into a blender and blend until smooth, add ice if you want a colder finish or if you want it more Frappe style.

Hey Mumma, has anyone told you that you're doing an excellent job?

Strawberry Sundae

2 Cups of frozen strawberries
1 Scoop of White Wolf Nutrition protein (I use Vanilla)
1/2 Cup of Greek yogurt
1 1/2 Cup of milk of your choice

Put all ingredients into a blender and blend until smooth, add ice if you want a colder finish or if you want it more Frappe style.

It's all very tough,
but so are you.

Acknowledgment

I'd like to take a moment to thank a few significant people in my life who made all this happen.

My daughter's father, Mitchell. Thank you for making me a mother and supporting Jordyn and I with everything we do. Thank you for jumping straight on board with this idea as soon as I even bought it up. Thank you for trusting me as a mother.

My parents, Bruce and Debbie Lorking. Thank you for everything you've done and continue to do for my family. Thank you for your continued support through everything I do.

My sister, Taylah Lorking. Thank you for being the first person to read the book and give me your honest opinion. Thank you for encouraging me to continue to work on it and thank you for loving my daughter almost as much as I do.

My cheerleaders, Tara, Hannah, Taylor, Maddie, Kath, and Emma. You ladies, are my ride or die. I wouldn't be the mother I was today if it wasn't for my ladies. Thank you for supporting me when I suggest crazy things like writing a book and for being the shoulder I cry on when I need it. I love you all so much, and you mean the world to me.

And Mel, the amazing coach at my gym. Thank you for being supportive of everything. Thank you for holding my sweet so I can have 45 minutes of uninterrupted training. You've done more for me than I can even describe. You're a big part of this book for me, you gave me the strength when things were hard.

Each and every one of you has such an important space in my heart, and you all love my daughter so much, which is an indescribable feeling. Thank you from the bottom of my heart for helping me reach my goal of writing a book. You're all fantastic.

About the Author

Courtney Lorking is the author behind Love yourself first, Mumma. She is a young mum who has had her struggles with mental health in the past. Dealing with depression and anxiety through her high school days and following into her life as an adult, she turned to health and fitness. She got her Personal Trainer certification in 2018 and has been obsessed with learning about all things wellness since. Courtney has seen first hand at what a whole lot of self-love and looking after your physical health can do for your mental health. Courtney calls the Central Coast, NSW, Australia, home.